4.99

W9-DDK-184

Marty Finds a Treasure

A Story About Prejudice

by Dorothy Fay Richards
illustrated by
Paul Karch

Published by The Dandelion House
A Division of The Child's World

Distributed by Childrens Press, 1224 West Van Buren Street, Chicago, Illinois 60607.

Library of Congress Cataloging in Publication Data

Richards, Dorothy Fay, 1915-
  Marty finds a treasure.

  (Making choices)
  Summary: When his father falls and breaks his leg in
an abandoned part of the city, the only person Marty
can find who is willing to help is a Latino.
  [1. Prejudice—Fiction] I. Karch, Paul, ill.
II. Title. III. Series.
PZ7.R379Mar 1983   [E]   82-19906
ISBN 0-89565-251-X

Published by The Dandelion House, A Division of The Child's World, Inc.
© 1982 SP Publications, Inc. Special revised edition, 1983.

1 2 3 4 5 6 7 8 9 10 11 12 R 89 88 87 86 85 84 83

Marty
Finds a
Treasure

THE CHILD'S WORLD

ELGIN, ILLINOIS 60120

In a certain city, there could be seen a group of old and empty buildings. There were tall apartment buildings that once had been fine places to live. There were stores that once had been nice places to visit. There were tumbled-down restaurants and broken-up streets.

Birds built nests on rotting beams; rats made homes under concrete piles; stray cats stalked around garbage heaps. People called the place Lost City.

No one lived in Lost City. But nearby, there were people. Many of them were Latinos who were new to the neighborhood. They spoke only Spanish. Many still dressed as they had in the country from which they came.

Some of the Latino kids were in Marty's school. Marty knew that his friends made fun of them and

called them mean names. Marty wondered why, but he'd never asked anyone. Marty didn't know much about these people, but he knew a lot about Lost City.

Marty and his father sometimes went to Lost City. They went to hunt for treasure with a metal detector. The detector gave off a beeping sound when it came near a metal object—even when the object was buried under the ground. Treasure-hunting was Mr. Clark's hobby. And it was Marty's favorite thing to do.

One summer Saturday, Marty suggested a trip to Lost City.

"Please, Dad? We don't have to stay long. We can be back before dark," coaxed Marty.

"Well," said Mr. Clark, folding his newspaper, "all right. You never know; this could be our day to discover something big!"

Mr. Clark went to the garage to get the metal detector. Marty grabbed their jackets.

Marty loved going to Lost City. Usually, he and his dad found only tin cans or buttons. But there was always a chance of finding money!

As Marty and his dad neared Lost City, Marty saw one of the kids from school. But Marty didn't call or wave. The boy was one of the Latinos. Marty wasn't sure why, but he thought he didn't like Latinos.

"Hey, Dad, over here!" Marty called as he climbed over a pile of broken bricks. "I found a new place!"

"And it's a good one," said his dad when he reached the spot. "There's a lot to explore here." He pointed the metal detector towards the ground as he walked.

"Beep, beep, beep . . ."

"Have we found something?" Marty asked.

"I don't know. But it's getting dark. We'll have to be careful!" Just then, Mr. Clark turned a corner.

"Ohhhhhhhhhhhhhh!" yelled Mr. Clark as he fell. Where there should have been steps, there were none. He had fallen into a basement.

Marty ran towards the sound. "Oh, Dad, are you hurt? Are you hurt?" he shouted from the edge of the hole.

"Marty, get back or you'll fall, too. . . I've hurt my leg. . . . Marty. . . . I think I'm going to faint. . . ." Mr. Clark's voice grew weaker and weaker and trailed off.

Marty's heart pounded. What could he do? There were no steps down into the hole.

"Dad?" Marty's voice echoed around him. This time there was no answer.

"I'll run for help," he thought. But then Marty thought, "What if I get lost? All these tall buildings— they all look alike. How will I find Dad again?"

Marty walked back and forth, trying to think. "Dad," he called. But still his dad didn't answer. Marty's heart beat so hard his chest hurt. And his hands were trembling.

"Maybe if I just go to that street over there," he finally decided, "I'll see someone. At least there are street lights there. And I can still find my way back to Dad. Yes, that's what I'll do."

Marty carefully looked upward, to see how the tall buildings were just where he stood. Then he walked from that spot to the edge of Lost City.

"Someone's bound to come by soon," he said to himself. "Someone has to!"

It was lonesome, standing so close to the ruins, with only bats zooming over his head for company. Marty stood there a long, long time. "I'd better go back and check on Dad," he said, finally.

But just then, he saw a man coming. He cupped his hands and shouted as loud as he could, "Hey — come over here and HELP me! HELP ME! HELP MY FATHER! HE CAN'T MOVE! HE HAS A BROKEN LEG!"

The man did not come any nearer. He did not change his fast walk. He waved his hand and yelled, "LATE — GOT TO HURRY!" Marty clenched his hands as the man turned a corner.

Marty ran back to his father. He had no problem finding the place. As he got close, he heard his father groaning.

"Never mind, Daddy! SOMEONE will help!" he said.

Marty hurried back to the through street and watched again for someone to pass by. Ahhhh — there was another man, at last.

Again Marty called, "PLEASE HELP! PLEASE HELP! MAN OVER HERE WITH A BROKEN LEG! PLEASE HELP!"

The man did not even slow up. He looked around fearfully. "You think I'm going to fall for that?" he said.

Marty burst into tears and twisted his hands in frustration. Was he going to stand here all night, and never find someone to help?

Again he ran back to his father. This time, Dad spoke to him. "I hope you get some help soon!" Mr. Clark said.

"I'm trying, Dad," Marty said and ran back to his watching-place. It seemed darker and colder. A wind had come up, and it whistled among the tall buildings. Marty felt lonelier and more helpless than ever.

Finally, there came another man, hurrying along. Marty could see that he was a Latino. But he called to him anyway.

"OVER HERE, OVER HERE! COME HELP MY FATHER. HE HAS A BROKEN LEG AND I CAN'T MOVE HIM! PLEASE HELP HIM!" His voice ended in a wail and a sob.

At first the man hesitated. He couldn't understand Marty's words. But when he saw that Marty was crying (the same sound in any language), he came running! Again Marty tried to explain with words what was wrong — no good. So he just took the man's sleeve and pulled him! The man nodded and walked with Marty.

Marty led the man back toward his father. The sun had set. Darkness was everywhere. The two had to walk very carefully now.

When they reached the hole, the man knelt and looked down. Then, grasping the edge, he swung himself over and dropped down. He knelt beside Mr. Clark.

"He doesn't speak English," Marty called, when his dad started explaining what had happened.

So Mr. Clark pointed to his leg. Gently, the man felt the leg, until Mr. Clark groaned. The man helped Mr. Clark to a more comfortable position against the wall. He spoke some quick words in Spanish, which Marty and Mr. Clark couldn't understand.

Then, with one hand he made the motions of dialing a telephone, while with the other, he held a receiver. Mr. Clark nodded, relieved.

The man climbed carefully out of the hole. He motioned for Marty to go down. Then the man ran down the street.

Marty sat down beside his father. His father reached out and took his hand.

"He's gone for help," Mr. Clark said. "There's nothing to do now but wait."

Within a few minutes, the man was back, with a team of paramedics. The paramedics lifted Mr. Clark out of the hole and put him on a stretcher. Marty rode in the ambulance with his dad. So did the Latino man.

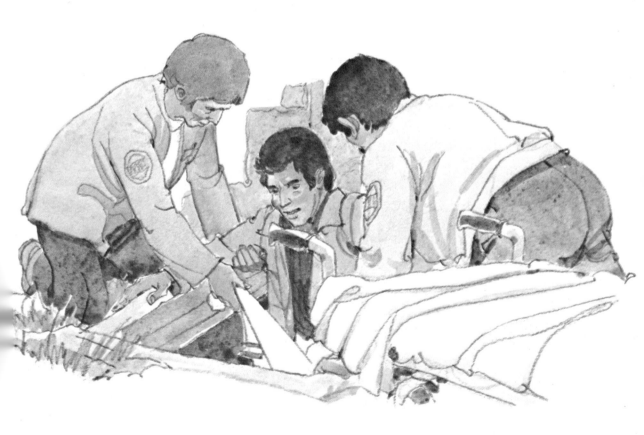

A doctor at the hospital could speak Spanish. He told Marty's new friend that Mr. Clark's leg was broken, but that he would be fine.

The man smiled and nodded. Marty gave him a hug. "Thank you," Marty said.

Again, the man seemed to understand. He waved to Marty as he left the hospital.

Later, as Marty sat next to his dad's bed, he asked why the Latino man had stopped to help when no one else would.

"He was kinder," said his dad, "and maybe not so scared. He was what we call a 'good neighbor'."

And then Marty's dad talked with Marty a long time. He explained about how looking different, and dressing different, and speaking a different language doesn't make a person good or bad. "We don't choose our friends for such reasons," said Mr. Clark.

"And learning that," he added, "is like finding a great treasure."

Marty nodded slowly. "I think I understand," he said.